CITIES THROUGH TIME

Paris

by Rebecca Sabelko
Illustrated by Diego Vaisberg

BLASTOFF! MISSIONS

BELLWETHER MEDIA
MINNEAPOLIS, MN

Blastoff! Missions takes you on a learning adventure! Colorful illustrations and exciting narratives highlight cool facts about our world and beyond. Read the mission goals and follow the narrative to gain knowledge, build reading skills, and have fun!

Traditional Nonfiction

Narrative Nonfiction

Blastoff! Universe

MISSION GOALS

> FIND YOUR SIGHT WORDS IN THE BOOK.

> LEARN ABOUT DIFFERENT PERIODS IN PARIS'S HISTORY.

> LEARN HOW DIFFERENT PEOPLE AND GROUPS CHANGED PARIS.

This edition first published in 2025 by Bellwether Media, Inc.

No part of this publication may be reproduced in whole or in part without written permission of the publisher. For information regarding permission, write to Bellwether Media, Inc., Attention: Permissions Department, 6012 Blue Circle Drive, Minnetonka, MN 55343.

Library of Congress Cataloging-in-Publication Data

LC record for Paris available at: https://lccn.loc.gov/2024021456

Text copyright © 2025 by Bellwether Media, Inc. BLASTOFF! MISSIONS and associated logos are trademarks and/or registered trademarks of Bellwether Media, Inc. Bellwether Media is a division of Chrysalis Education Group.

Editor: Christina Leaf   Designer: Laura Sowers

Printed in the United States of America, North Mankato, MN.

This is **Blastoff Jimmy**! He is here to help you on your mission and share fun facts along the way!

Table of Contents

Welcome to Paris!	4
Built on an Island	6
A Growing City	10
The City Today	20
Glossary	22
To Learn More	23
Beyond the Mission	24
Index	24

Welcome to Paris!

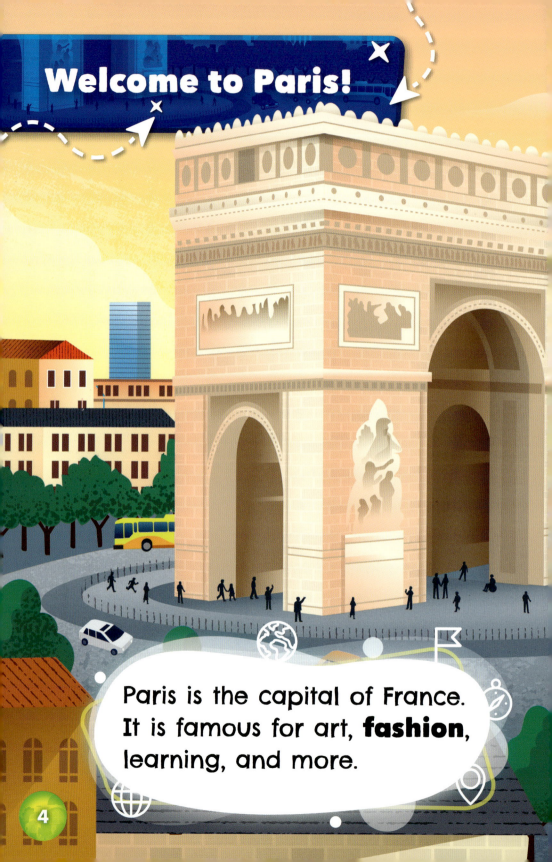

Paris is the capital of France. It is famous for art, **fashion**, learning, and more.

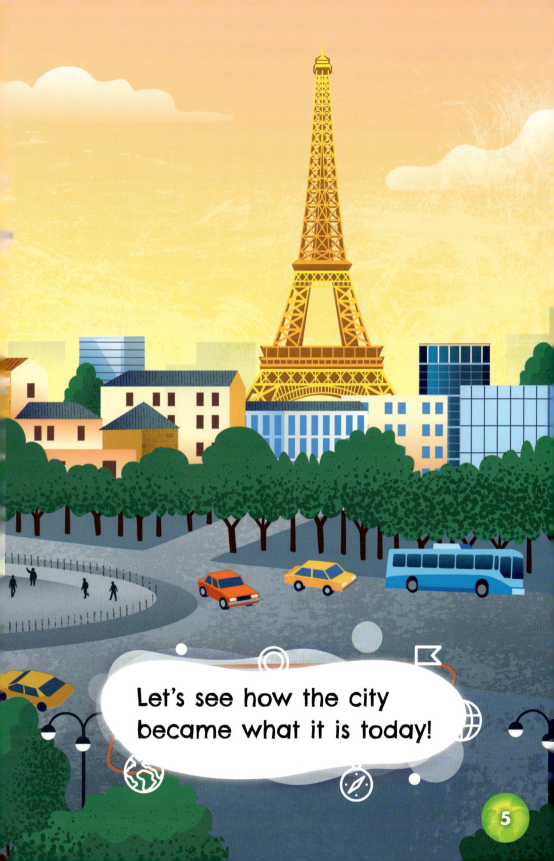

A Growing City

early 1200s

There is a lot happening in Paris! People **trade** goods on the Seine's right bank.

Leaders work on the island. Students study at **colleges** along the river's left bank.

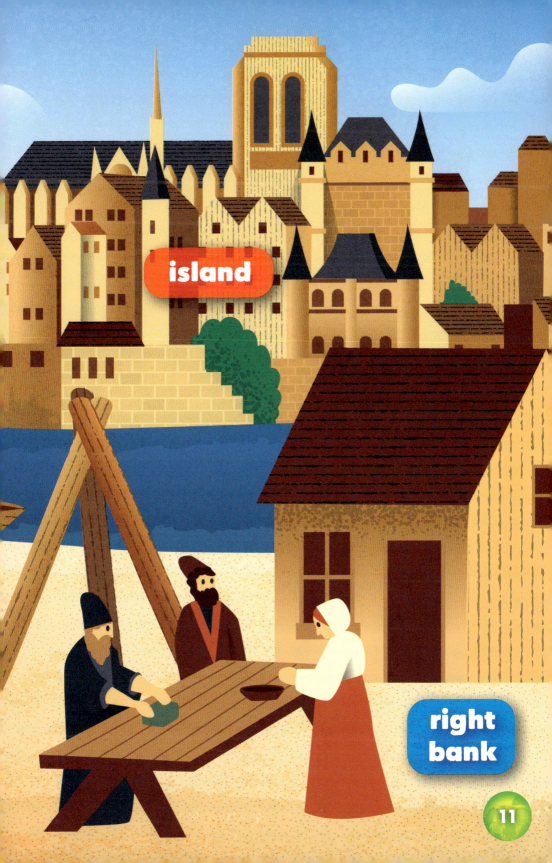

July 14, 1789

The people of Paris are attacking the Bastille **Fortress**! It is the start of a **revolution**.

France's people want more rights. Will they gain freedom?

The City Today

today

Paris is a top city for **culture** and learning. People visit museums. They meet at cafés.

Travelers enjoy seeing the city's rich history come alive!

Paris Timeline

200s BCE: The Parisii live in a fishing village on the Seine River

100s CE: Romans grow the city of Lutetia that will later become Paris

early 1200s: Paris is a major city for trade, government, and learning

July 14, 1789: Parisians attack the Bastille, starting the French Revolution

1871 to 1914: Paris has a boom of art and architecture during the "beautiful era"

1889: The Eiffel Tower is completed for the World's Fair

1947: Christian Dior's first fashion show takes place in Paris

Paris, France

21

Glossary

amphitheater–a round, outdoor theater with many levels of seats

colleges–schools for higher learning

culture–the beliefs, arts, and ways of life in a place or society

fashion–related to styles of clothing

fortress–a building or place from which people can prevent attacks

forum–a marketplace or public place in a Roman city

revolution–a sudden change in government

trade–to buy and sell

World War II–the war fought from 1939 to 1945 that involved many countries

To Learn More

AT THE LIBRARY

Gleisner, Jenna Lee. *My First Look at French.* Minneapolis, Minn.: Jump!, 2020.

Leaf, Christina. *Rome.* Minneapolis, Minn.: Bellwether Media, 2024.

Sabelko, Rebecca. *France.* Minneapolis, Minn.: Bellwether Media, 2023.

ON THE WEB

FACTSURFER

Factsurfer.com gives you a safe, fun way to find more information.

1. Go to www.factsurfer.com.

2. Enter "Paris" into the search box and click 🔍.

3. Select your book cover to see a list of related content.

BEYOND THE MISSION

> WHAT FACT FROM THE BOOK DID YOU THINK WAS THE MOST INTERESTING?

> WHICH POINT IN PARIS'S HISTORY WOULD YOU WANT TO VISIT? WHY?

> PRETEND YOU ARE A FASHION DESIGNER IN PARIS IN 1947. DRAW YOUR DESIGNS FOR A FASHION SHOW.

Index

amphitheater, 9
art, 4, 14
Bastille Fortress, 12, 13
beautiful era, 15
café, 14, 20
capital, 4
colleges, 10
culture, 20
Dior, Christian, 18
Eiffel Tower, 16, 17
fashion, 4, 18
forum, 8, 9
France, 4, 13

island, 6, 7, 8, 10, 11
learning, 4, 20
Lutetia, 8
Parisii, 6
people, 6, 10, 13, 16, 17, 18, 19, 20
revolution, 13
Romans, 8
Seine River, 6, 7, 10
timeline, 21
trade, 10
World War II, 19
World's Fair, 16